MW01521045

The Great Depression

Joy Gregory and John Willis

LIGHTB◆X
openlightbox.com

LIGHTBOX

Go to
www.openlightbox.com
and enter this book's
unique code.

ACCESS CODE

L B X 7 9 7 9 5

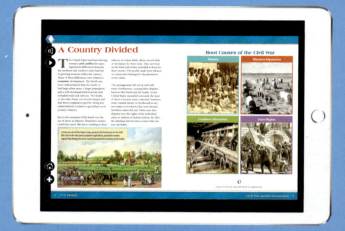

Lightbox is an all-inclusive digital solution for the teaching and learning of curriculum topics in an original, groundbreaking way. Lightbox is based on National Curriculum Standards.

STANDARD FEATURES OF LIGHTBOX

 AUDIO High-quality narration using text-to-speech system

 ACTIVITIES Printable PDFs that can be emailed and graded

 SLIDESHOWS Pictorial overviews of key concepts

VIDEOS Embedded high-definition video clips

 WEBLINKS Curated links to external, child-safe resources

 TRANSPARENCIES Step-by-step layering of maps, diagrams, charts, and timelines

 INTERACTIVE MAPS Interactive maps and aerial satellite imagery

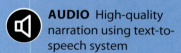

 QUIZZES Ten multiple choice questions that are automatically graded and emailed for teacher assessment

 KEY WORDS Matching key concepts to their definitions

Copyright © 2017 Smartbook Media Inc. All rights reserved.

Contents

Writing a Comparative Essay

Teacher Preplanning

Students will analyze two topics, and then write a comparative essay based on their analysis. An exemplary comparative essay will meet the following criteria.

- Consists of a one-paragraph introduction, two or more body paragraphs, and a one-paragraph conclusion
- Introduction includes an engaging lead statement about the topic of the essay, more detailed information about the chosen topic, and a one-sentence thesis that specifically states the essay's argument
- Each body paragraph includes a topic sentence that refers to and supports the thesis, textual evidence of the argument, and an analysis of this evidence
- Body paragraphs end with a transition to the next paragraph
- Conclusion refers to the topic of the essay and the points presented in the body paragraphs, and restates the thesis
- Provides a thorough analysis of the topics in question
- Presents a clear, specific thesis that indicates a high level of critical engagement
- Organizes ideas in a logical manner
- Communicates arguments in a clear, effective manner
- Uses correct spelling, punctuation, and grammar
- Properly integrates any quotations used
- Correctly cites all sources used
- Correctly formats bibliography

A False Prosperity

Known as the Roaring Twenties, the decade from 1920 to 1929 was a time of great optimism in the United States. The country had been on the winning side in World War I, which ended in 1918, and had emerged from the war as a major world power. Americans were confident about the strength of their country and its **economy**.

To many Americans, the 1920s was a time of excitement and possibility. Families gathered around their new radios and went to the movies. People listened to jazz, a new type of music created by African Americans, who brought it to northern cities from the South. Women, who were given the right to vote in 1920, wore shorter skirts and enjoyed more free time as a result of the invention of household appliances such as vacuum cleaners and washing machines. Automobiles were becoming popular.

Many Americans could afford these new products as a result of the country's financial **prosperity**. People living in cities were earning more money than ever before, and few workers were unemployed. With more people able to buy **consumer goods**, businesses produced more. In the years from 1919 to 1929, U.S. industrial production grew by 30 percent.

Not everyone shared in the wealth. Many families earned less than the amount required to meet their basic needs of food, shelter, and clothing. In addition, farmers earned much less than city workers. Even so, confidence in the future dominated the U.S. economy.

By 1929, "Blue Skies," written by Irving Berlin, was the most popular song in the country. The lyrics promised "nothing but blue skies from now on." That hopefulness was shared by the Republican president, Herbert Hoover, who was elected in 1928. Many believed the nation had entered a period of permanent prosperity. However, that was not to be the case. In 1929, the Great Depression would begin. This period of severe economic hardship, often referred to as just the Depression, would last until 1939.

City dwellers in the 1920s had more leisure time to enjoy activities such as going to the beach.

Root Causes of the Great Depression

An Unsound Stock Market

Overproduction of Consumer Goods

Agricultural Problems

A Faulty Banking System

EXTENSION ACTIVITY

Analyzing an Advertisement

Teacher Preplanning
Students will choose a video or print advertisement and analyze it critically. An exemplary analysis will meet the following criteria.

- Identifies what product the advertisement is trying to sell
- Determines when and where the advertisement was created
- Identifies who the advertisement is targeted towards
- Describes any figures that appear in the advertisement
- Discusses any themes that are present in the advertisement
- Determines the usage of tools such as humor to sell a product
- Summarizes any plot or story found in the advertisement
- Differentiates between facts and other statements used by the advertiser.
- Infers advertising strategies based on content
- Cites all sources used in the analysis
- Uses correct spelling, grammar, and punctuation

The 1920s were a carefree time for many in the United States. Young city-dwellers enjoyed using their wages to socialize with others in local clubs.

Looming Trouble

The Great Depression was largely rooted in the economic policies of the 1920s. Warren G. Harding, Calvin Coolidge, and Herbert Hoover were the three Republican presidents elected in that decade. They were all guided by the idea that the U.S., or federal, government should not regulate the economy.

In the years leading up to 1929, federal policies encouraged the development of private businesses and discouraged government oversight of financial matters, including banks and the stock market.

There was no system in place to deal with unsound banks and a stock market in danger of collapsing. The government also played no role in controlling manufacturing or agricultural production.

Many changes took place in the United States during the 1920s. That decade marked the first time in U.S. history that more people lived in cities than on farms. When World War I ended, many young men returning from Europe took jobs in cities rather than settling on family farms or in rural communities. Many women who had taken factory and other jobs to aid the war effort decided to keep working. The result was a significant increase in the number city dwellers who earned cash wages and were ready to spend.

The population as a whole was eager to buy products that had been in short supply during the war. The U.S. economy moved from producing goods for the war effort to manufacturing a wide range of consumer goods, from automobiles to ready-made clothing. Not everyone could afford to buy these new products, so companies began selling goods on credit. Consumers would make a small payment, take home the product, and continue to pay for it in installments over a period of time. Credit was also used to buy stock in the stock market. The practice of purchasing stock using mostly borrowed money is known as buying on margin. Banks, too, invested in the stock market, using money that consumers had **deposited**.

Farmers borrowed money to buy new machinery and land, on which they grew more and more crops. The **surplus** led to lower prices, and farmers had trouble paying back their loan. This hurt small rural banks. Companies and individuals also began to struggle to pay their debts. Despite the appearance of prosperity, by 1929, more than 60 percent of American families earned less than $2,000 per year, and more than 40 percent earned less than $1,500. This was at a time when $2,500 was considered necessary to support a family.

Norman Rockwell and the *Saturday Evening Post*

Between 1916 and 1965, paintings by artist Norman Rockwell appeared on the cover of the *Saturday Evening Post* 321 times. The *Saturday Evening Post* was a popular national magazine that portrayed the 1920s as a time in which people lived glamorous, exciting lives. Rockwell was known for images of life in America, and his covers during the 1920s showed confident, happy Americans.

The magazine featured advertisements for factory-made products such as household appliances, soap, clothing, and automobiles. Rockwell created the illustrations for many of these products. The companies selling the goods placed the ads to attract young city dwellers with money to spend. These consumers were eager to purchase the products. They believed that the products would make their lives more exciting and interesting.

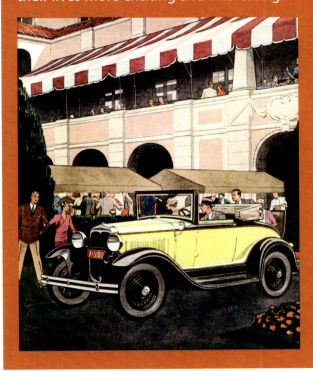

TEACHER NOTES

🗎 Document

Saturday Evening Post Covers and Ads
Review and discuss various images created by Norman Rockwell for the *Saturday Evening Post*.

1. What tools does Rockwell use in his illustrations to sell a product to the viewer? Why would these be effective marketing strategies?
2. How are these advertisements different from modern ones? How are they similar?
3. How do Rockwell's covers differ from his advertisements? How are they similar? What are some possible reasons for these differences and similarities?

🌐 Weblink

The Charleston
Examine the history of the Charleston dance and the impact that it had on society during the Roaring Twenties.

1. Why was the Charleston so popular? How does this relate to attitudes during the Roaring Twenties?
2. How did the Charleston come to represent the emancipation of women? Why was it also considered a symbol of the Jazz Age? Why might the dance have earned the disapproval of some people?

Creating a Timeline

Teacher Preplanning

Students will explore a topic related to a historical event and create a timeline to present their research on historical events connected to this topic. An exemplary timeline will meet the following criteria.

- Includes the most significant events pertaining to the topic to be compared and analyzed
- Includes interesting events
- Uses accurate information for all events, including date, location, and major details
- Orders the events in a chronological sequence
- Describes each event with accurate, vivid, and specific details
- Presents the topic from three or more perspectives
- Inspires the reader to ask thoughtful questions regarding the events and perspectives presented in the timeline
- Uses correct spelling, grammar, and punctuation
- Presents the timeline in a visually attractive and striking manner
- Presents the timeline in a neat, organized manner that is logical and easy to follow
- Uses creativity to present the timeline in an engaging manner
- Effectively communicates historical information relating to the topic
- Supports each event with reliable sources
- Includes a correctly formatted bibliography of all sources used to create the timeline

Timeline of the Great Depression

★ **October 29, 1929** On what becomes known as Black Tuesday, share prices on the New York Stock Exchange drop sharply. Over the next few weeks, the value of stocks drops by more than $30 billion, an event known as a stock market crash.

★ **Summer 1930** A **drought** begins in the central United States. Drought conditions will continue throughout the 1930s.

★ **September 1931** The first major **dust storm** sweeps across parts of Texas, Oklahoma, Kansas, Nebraska, Colorado, and New Mexico, a region that becomes known as the Dust Bowl.

★ **July 2, 1932** Franklin D. Roosevelt accepts the Democratic Party's presidential nomination and promises a "new deal for the American people."

★ **July 28, 1932** U.S. troops fire on the Bonus Army, a group of World War I veterans camped in Washington, D.C., demanding bonuses they were promised by the government.

★ **November 8, 1932** Roosevelt is elected president in a landslide, or by a wide margin.

★ **March 5, 1933** The day after he is sworn in as president, Roosevelt calls for a "Bank Holiday," closing the nation's banks for several days.

★ **March 9, 1933** Beginning what becomes known as the 100 Days, measures suggested by Roosevelt are passed by Congress to deal with the Depression. In the next months, New Deal programs such as the Agricultural Adjustment Act, Tennessee Valley Authority (TVA), National Industrial Recovery Act, and Public Works Administration are established.

★ **March 12, 1933** Roosevelt delivers the first "fireside chat," using a national radio broadcast to talk to the American people from the White House and explain new banking laws.

★ **December 5, 1933** Prohibition, a nationwide ban on the manufacture and sale of alcoholic beverages, ends with the ratification of the 21ˢᵗ Amendment to the U.S. Constitution.

★ **August 14, 1935** The Social Security Act is signed into law, providing cash payments for older people, the disabled, and the unemployed.

★ **June 25, 1938** The Fair Labor Standards Act is signed into law, setting a **minimum wage** and limiting the number of hours per week a person could be required to work.

★ **September 1, 1939** World War II begins in Europe, and the United States starts to sell weapons and other materials to its allies. The shift to wartime production eventually ends the Great Depression.

Leading the Country

Analyzing a Historical Biography

Teacher Preplanning

Students will research the life of a historical figure and present their findings. An exemplary biographical analysis will meet the following criteria.

- Illustrates strong knowledge of the subject
- Identifies the author of the biography
- Describes why the subject of the biography is important
- Contains information about the time and place in which the subject was born
- Lists important events in the subject's life
- Explains how events in the subject's life impacted him or her
- Makes inferences about the subject based on events in his or her life
- Explains how the subject influenced the world while he or she lived
- Researches the cultural and historical context of the subject's life
- Examines the effect that the subject has had on the modern world
- Supplements information from the biography with independent research
- Organizes the analysis in a logical, effective manner
- Uses correct spelling, grammar, and punctuation
- Cites all sources used in the analysis

Two presidents led the United States during the years of the Great Depression. Each approached the country's economic problems with different ideas about the federal government's role in the economy.

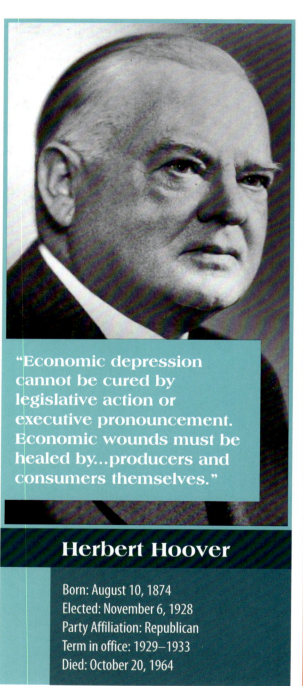

"Economic depression cannot be cured by legislative action or executive pronouncement. Economic wounds must be healed by...producers and consumers themselves."

Herbert Hoover

Born: August 10, 1874
Elected: November 6, 1928
Party Affiliation: Republican
Term in office: 1929–1933
Died: October 20, 1964

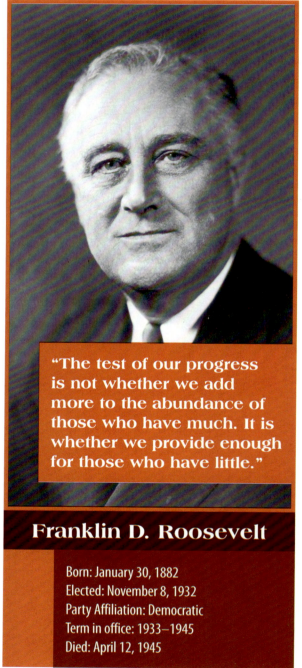

"The test of our progress is not whether we add more to the abundance of those who have much. It is whether we provide enough for those who have little."

Franklin D. Roosevelt

Born: January 30, 1882
Elected: November 8, 1932
Party Affiliation: Democratic
Term in office: 1933–1945
Died: April 12, 1945

While Hoover favored a limited role, Roosevelt believed the government had to take action. He was aided by advisers who shared this view, including members of his **cabinet** and his wife, who became one of the most active first ladies of all time.

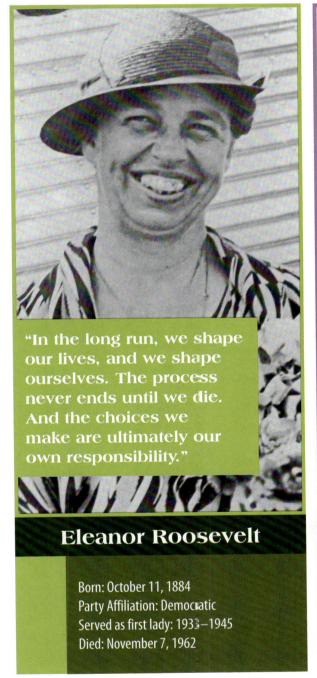

"In the long run, we shape our lives, and we shape ourselves. The process never ends until we die. And the choices we make are ultimately our own responsibility."

Eleanor Roosevelt

Born: October 11, 1884
Party Affiliation: Democratic
Served as first lady: 1933–1945
Died: November 7, 1962

"The people are what matter to government, and a government should aim to give all the people under its jurisdiction the best possible life."

Frances Perkins

Born: April 10, 1880
Party Affiliation: Democratic
Sworn in as secretary of labor: March 4, 1933
Served in Roosevelt's cabinet: 1933–1945
Died: May 14, 1965

© **More**

Great Depression Biographies
Examine the lives of important historical figures during the Great Depression. Discuss the ways in which they have influenced both historical and modern events.

1. How might each figure's background have influenced his or her career path?
2. What role did these people play in guiding the country through the Great Depression? Were their contributions effective at the time? Why or why not?
3. What impact did their contributions during the Great Depression have on the United States today? How would the country be different if their contributions had not occurred?

The Great Depression 11

The Depression Begins

Today, historians and economists debate whether the stock market crash of 1929 actually started the Great Depression or just increased the severity of financial problems that had existed for some time. In any case, the New York Stock Exchange crash generally is viewed as the beginning of the Depression, which became the most serious and longest-lasting economic **recession** ever experienced in the Western world.

A year before the crash, some financial experts feared a stock market collapse was likely to occur. In a healthy market, companies sold shares in their business to raise cash, which would be used to expand their enterprises and make more money.

That tied stock prices to what a company was worth. By 1928, however, stock prices were rising because of buyer demand, not corporate value. In other words, share prices rose because so many people wanted to buy stocks. The fact that many people used borrowed money to buy their shares added to the risk. If stock prices fell, many of these borrowers would be unable to repay their loans.

The economy had already begun to slow by 1929, as fewer people bought goods and unemployment rose somewhat. Then, in September 1929, stock prices began to fall. On Thursday, October 24, many people began to sell their shares, concerned about the falling prices. Investors panicked as

Huge crowds gathered outside the New York Stock Exchange as word spread about the crash of the stock market.

prices continued to fall. By the middle of the day, a group of wealthy bankers gathered and took action to avoid a collapse of the market. They began buying shares, which stopped prices from falling.

By Monday, October 28, it was clear that the market was in trouble again. Losses mounted, and by the end of the day, the market had lost more than 12 percent of its value. The next day, "Black Tuesday," people continued to panic and sell their shares, causing the market to crash. Billions of dollars were lost, and millions of individuals and companies were financially ruined. The Great Depression had begun.

In 1929, **$2 of every $5** loaned by banks were used to buy stocks.

On Black Tuesday, a record **16 million shares** were traded on the New York Stock Exchange. Shares of the 16 largest companies lost close to **$3 billion**.

"Brother, Can You Spare a Dime?"

In 1930, two New York songwriters named E. Y. "Yip" Harburg and Jay Gorney wrote a song called "Brother, Can You Spare a Dime?" It became the anthem of the Great Depression, a song that captured the suffering of many people during this time. Other songs of the period were about believing that things would get better, but this song was different.

With lyrics that described sadness and despair, "Brother, Can You Spare a Dime?" expressed the country's loss of optimism in the early years of the Depression. Specific verses voiced the difficulties of former soldiers who had served in World War I and unemployed workers who needed to beg for money and felt forgotten by a nation they helped build. Singer Bing Crosby recorded the song in 1932, and it became a national hit.

📄 **Document**

Brother, Can You Spare a Dime
Listen to and read the lyrics of the song "Brother, Can You Spare a Dime," and examine it as a product of the Great Depression.

1. What specific historical events do the song's lyrics reference? How are they used to further the song's message?
2. How do the songwriter and singer express emotion in the song? What emotional impact does this have on a listener?
3. How do this song's tone and content compare to that or more recent hit music? What are some possible reasons for any similarities or differences?

👁 **First Hand**

The Wall Street Crash, 1929
Examine one reporter's account of the events on and surrounding Black Tuesday.

1. How did different corporations attempt to prevent the stock market crash from occurring? Why were these efforts unsuccessful? What other strategies could have been employed to try to turn the situation around?
2. How did individuals react to the market collapse? What factors may have influenced these specific reactions? What do these reactions say about the mindset of the time?

Making Do

By the early 1930s, millions of Americans had lost their jobs, and a severe drought was making it impossible for many farmers to grow crops to sell. People could not afford to buy ready-made clothes or needed household items. They adopted the motto "repair, reuse, make do, and don't throw anything away."

REPURPOSED CURTAINS

SACK DRESSES

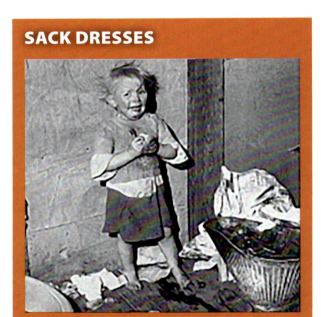

ZIPPERS

REPAIRED SHOES

DARNED SOCKS

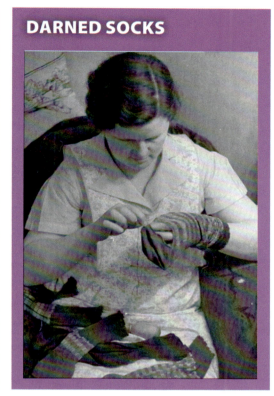

CARDBOARD

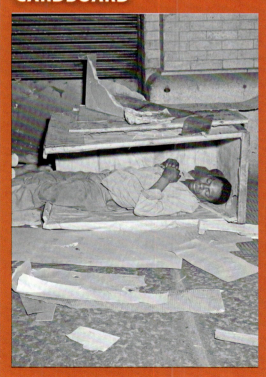

NEWSPAPERS

The Crisis Spreads

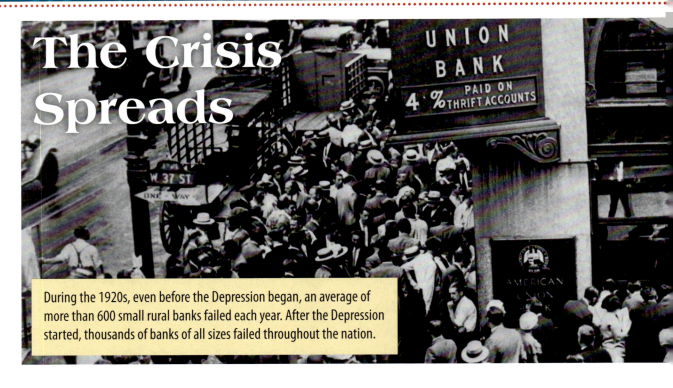

During the 1920s, even before the Depression began, an average of more than 600 small rural banks failed each year. After the Depression started, thousands of banks of all sizes failed throughout the nation.

The stock market crisis pushed the struggling U.S. economy to the point of disaster. Banks needed to make up for their own stock losses. To do so, they demanded that people and businesses who had borrowed from them repay the loans. At the same time, anxious people withdrew the money they had deposited in banks. In just the last two months of 1929, these "bank panics" caused about 650 banks to fail, or close because they did not have enough money to continue operating. Another 1,300 banks closed the next year. The number of people out of work also increased sharply. In 1929, the national **unemployment rate** was 3.1 percent. In 1930, it rose to 8.7 percent.

On June 17, 1930, President Hoover signed the Smoot-Hawley **Tariff** Act, which had been passed by Congress. The law raised taxes on thousands of imported products brought in from other nations. The intention was to help U.S. businesses sell more by making competing foreign goods more expensive. However, the act also hurt U.S. businesses and farms. Foreign nations, struggling with their own economic downturns, raised their tariffs on U.S. goods. The result was that foreign demand for U.S. products, including agricultural goods, fell. With prices low and other countries buying fewer crops from the United States, American farmers could not pay their bills or make payments on their loans.

Farmers' problems became worse when a drought began in 1930. About 150,000 square miles of land in the central and western United States received little rain or snow for a number of years. The soil became so dry that crops could not grow. In many

areas, soil turned to dust. Beginning in 1931, a series of wind storms, called "black blizzards," blew through the region, taking the topsoil away. There were 14 storms in 1932 and 38 the next year in the Dust Bowl region. At times, people and livestock died from inhaling dust.

Unable to grow crops or make money, millions of people left the region in search of jobs. Many set out for California, where they thought there might be work. They traveled along Route 66, a 2,450-mile stretch of road that linked Chicago, Illinois, and Los Angeles, California. Route 66 passed through Missouri, Kansas, Oklahoma, Texas, New Mexico, and Arizona, some of the states most severely affected by the dust storms. Those who went west were called Okies, even if they were not from Oklahoma.

The Dust Bowl Folk Singer

Woodrow Wilson Guthrie, known as Woody, was an American folk singer and songwriter. Born in 1912 in Okemah, Oklahoma, Guthrie traveled around the country and went west to California during the 1930s. As Guthrie too had been forced to leave his home, he understood what other Okies were experiencing. Guthrie is best known for songs such as "Talkin' Dust Bowl Blues," "Dust Bowl Refugee," and "This Land Is Your Land." His songs told of the struggles so many people experienced during the Great Depression.

Guthrie died in 1967. Many of his songs are still sung today. He inspired a number of later artists, including Bob Dylan, Bruce Springsteen, and his son Arlo Guthrie.

TEACHER NOTES

 **Document**

Woodrow Wilson Guthrie Lyrics
Analyze the lyrics to "This Land" and "Talking Dust Bowl Blues" and the ways in which they relate the difficulties faced during the Great Depression.

1. What tone or tones do the songs take? How and why does the tone change over the course of each song?
2. What imagery does Guthrie use to illustrate the events of the Great Depression? Is the imagery effective? In what way?
3. What emotional responses are the songs trying to evoke? Are they successful? Why or why not?

 Weblink

Okie Migrations
Examine an overview of the mass migration to states such as California during the Great Depression.

1. What factors led people to move west? Why did they choose the destinations that they did? Would this have been a wise decision in the long-term? Why or why not?
2. How did locals react to the influx of "Okies"? What are some reasons why they would have reacted in the way that they did? How justified were they in their reactions?

Mapping the Great Depression

The Great Depression affected people across the United States. Unemployment was high everywhere but worse in some states. Some areas were also hit especially hard by drought. After Roosevelt became president, many new government programs sought to improve conditions. The TVA built dams and generated electricity for areas near the Tennessee River. Other **public works programs** gave people jobs constructing roads, bridges, parks, and public buildings. Artists were employed painting murals to decorate those buildings.

This map indicates the depth of the Depression across the nation and some significant public works projects.

1. Grand Coulee Dam

2. Coit Tower

3. Hoover Dam

4. Voice of America Building

5. LaGuardia Airport

6. Bethesda Post Office

PACIFIC OCEAN

MEXICO

Legend

- States with unemployment rates over 30% (1933)
- States with unemployment rates under 30% (1933)
- Dust Bowl region
- Tennessee Valley Authority region

0 — 250 Miles

N

CANADA
North Dakota
South Dakota
Minnesota
Wisconsin
Michigan
Vermont
Maine
New York
New Hampshire
Massachusetts
Rhode Island
Connecticut
Pennsylvania
New Jersey
Nebraska
Iowa
Illinois
Indiana
Ohio
Kansas
Missouri
West Virginia
Virginia
Delaware
Maryland
Kentucky
Tennessee
North Carolina
Oklahoma
Arkansas
South Carolina
Texas
Alabama
Georgia
Mississippi
Louisiana
Florida
ATLANTIC OCEAN
GULF OF MEXICO
THE BAHAMAS
CUBA
4
5
6

TEACHER NOTES

Google Maps

Mapping the Great Depression

Explore the sites of several structures built as public works projects during the Great Depression using street view.

1. What impact would these public works projects have had on the area and the people living there at the time?
2. How worthwhile were the projects in the long term? What role do they play in the United States today?
3. Which of these structures has been the most useful to the country as a whole? Why did you choose that structure?

Hardship and Violence

In early 1931, food riots began to occur in parts of the United States. In Oklahoma City, Oklahoma, in January, a crowd of unemployed men and women raided a grocery store. The next month, in Minneapolis, Minnesota, hundreds of people broke the windows of a grocery store and stole food, and the store owner shot at the looters.

The unemployment rate in 1931 reached 15.8 percent, and some Americans were becoming desperate. Banks continued to fail throughout the year. Bank panics occurred in September, when 305 banks closed, and October, when 522 closed.

A growing number of banks in the Midwest closed after farmers and other landowners **defaulted** on their loans. Rural banks **foreclosed** on land and equipment but then had difficulty auctioning them off to obtain cash. In 1931, farmers in Madison County, Nebraska, staged what became known as the first Penny Auction. When bank agents asked for bids on land and equipment being auctioned, farmers made a few very low bids and then prevented people from placing higher bids.

To give farmers a chance to pay back their loans, some states passed laws that delayed farm foreclosures by up to a year. State government officials assumed that the Depression would end soon and that farmers would be able to pay their loans in time. However, economic conditions did not improve. When the year ran out, farm foreclosures continued.

President Hoover, believing that people should not depend on the government for help, called for business and industry to cooperate to put people back to work and keep wages high for those who were still employed. He asked private charities to aid the needy. Hoover repeatedly told the American people that "prosperity is just around the corner." He announced that state and local efforts that had been set up were enough to provide relief for those in need. The president believed that the Depression would end soon.

The collapse of the Bank of the United States in New York in December 1930 was the largest-ever failure of a single bank. It **lost more than $200 million in deposits**.

In 1920, farmers could sell a bushel of wheat for **$2.94**. By 1932, the price had dropped to **$0.30**.

Los Angeles was one of a number of American cities in which food riots took place.

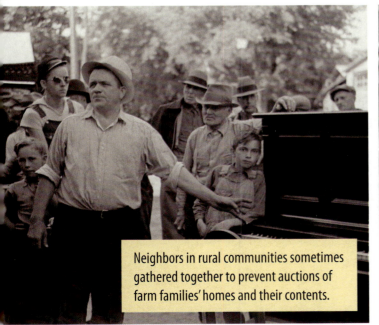

Neighbors in rural communities sometimes gathered together to prevent auctions of farm families' homes and their contents.

Some unemployed people bought apples on credit from a fruit supplier. They then sold the apples on street corners for 5 cents.

👁 First Hand

Fending off Foreclosures with Penny Auctions

Review an interview discussing the events that led to penny auctions as a method used to prevent farms from being foreclosed by banks.

1. Why was this topic considered relevant in 2007? Is it still relevant today? Why or why not?
2. Why would banks have called Minnesota's governor a bolshevik for calling a moratorium on farm foreclosures? Why would other people refer to him as a hero?
3. Why were the penny auctions of the Great Depression so effective? How effective would this form of protest be today? Why?

▶ Video

History Brief: Herbert Hoover

Examine an analysis of President Hoover's life and role during the Great Depression.

1. In what ways might Hoover's experiences during the First World War have influenced his strategies during the Great Depression?
2. How did Hoover attempt to counteract the Great Depression? Why might these attempts have failed? Are there any alternate strategies that would have had a more positive effect?
3. How is President Hoover remembered today? How would this differ from the ways in which people thought of him during and shortly after the Great Depression? Why?

Analyzing Famous Speeches as Arguments

Teacher Preplanning
Students will analyze a well-known speech as an argument and write a response. An exemplary analysis will meet the following criteria.

- Presents a strong thesis that is based on analysis of the argument presented in the speech
- Consistently uses strong textual evidence to support the thesis
- Presents an engaging and effective introduction, body, and conclusion
- Structures the analysis in a logical order
- Uses clear prose to present the student's voice and perspective
- Identifies the main points presented in the speech
- Identifies the speaker and infers how his or her life may have shaped this argument
- Identifies when and where the speech was given
- Determines the speech's intended audience
- Analyzes how the speaker makes his or her argument
- Uses strong evidence from the speech to show how the speaker supports his or her argument
- Analyzes the language used to convey the speech's argument
- Demonstrates understanding of the historical and societal context in which the speech was given and connects that context to the speaker's argument
- Properly integrates quotations
- Properly cites all sources used

The Promise of a New Deal

By 1932, more than 23 percent of U.S. workers, or 12 million people, were unemployed. President Hoover realized that conditions were more serious than he had originally thought. He created the Reconstruction Finance Corporation. This government agency began making loans to banks, railroads, and other businesses to help them continue operating and employ workers. Some public works projects were funded, as well as housing projects built with government money. At its convention in June, the Republican Party nominated Hoover to run for reelection.

The Democratic Party nominated New York governor Franklin Roosevelt as its candidate. During the campaign, Roosevelt blamed the Republicans and their policies for the collapse of the stock market. He promised that he would fight the economic downturn with a series of federal programs, a "New Deal," to help American workers and farmers.

During the campaign, a group of jobless World War I veterans known as the Bonus Army marched on Washington, D.C. Years earlier, the government had promised that it would give the veterans benefits, or cash

The Bonus Army hoped to convince Congress to pass a bill to pay benefits early. The House of Representatives voted in favor of the bill, but the Senate turned it down.

payments. However, the benefits were scheduled to be paid in 1945. Thousands of veterans, some with family members, camped outside the Capitol building and demanded that the bonuses be paid immediately. Hoover was afraid the veterans would riot, and on July 28, Army troops fired on them to make them leave. Several of the veterans were injured. Americans were shocked to learn of these events. Several months later, on November 8, Roosevelt won the election with more than 57 percent of the vote.

Franklin Roosevelt's New Deal Speech

On July 2, 1932, Roosevelt established a new tradition by flying to Chicago, Illinois, to appear at the Democratic National Convention to accept the party's nomination in person. Before this, no presidential candidate had ever appeared in person to accept nomination at a convention. Acknowledging the "unprecedented and unusual times" facing the nation, Roosevelt used his acceptance speech to set the foundation for the New Deal. In the speech, he detailed the need for the federal government to take direct action in the economy. He did not discuss specific steps he would take and may not have even known at the time what he would do once he became president. However, Roosevelt talked about putting the unemployed to work, making changes in the country's banking system, and aiding farmers.

"I pledge you, I pledge myself, to a new deal for the American people."

Franklin Roosevelt

Roosevelt set up a team of advisers, known as the Brain Trust, who helped him develop the economic policies followed in the New Deal.

The First 100 Days

Roosevelt was sworn into office on March 4, 1933. The first months of his presidency, a period that became known as the 100 Days, were a time of swift action. Roosevelt used **executive orders** for some policies, and he also convinced Congress to pass 15 major laws to deal with the effects of the Depression and improve the economy.

To stop people from withdrawing money from the banks that still existed, the president ordered all U.S. banks to close for four days, beginning March 6. During that time, Congress passed the Emergency Banking Act, which allowed banks to reopen under the supervision of the Treasury Department once they had shown that they were financially sound. This helped to bring back public confidence in the banking system. On March 12, 60 million Americans listened to a radio broadcast in which the president told them how the government was dealing with the nation's banking problem. This speech was the first of 27 fireside chats that Roosevelt gave during his administration to communicate directly with the public and provide encouragement.

The Persistence of Unemployment

The rate of unemployment was extremely low during the 1920s. However, the rate rose sharply when the Depression began. Unemployment was one of the most serious problems faced during the Great Depression.

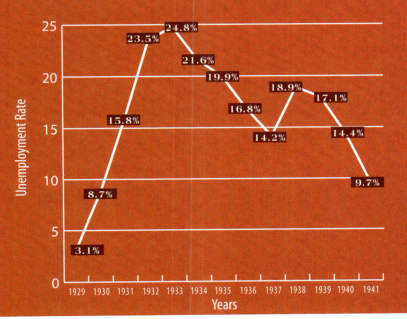

Document

Fireside Chat on Banking
Examine a transcript of Roosevelt's first fireside chat, discussing the bank holiday that was taking place at the time.

1. What is the tone of the speech? Why might Roosevelt be speaking in this manner?
2. What goal is Roosevelt trying to accomplish? How successful is he at achieving this goal? Why?
3. Why would Roosevelt continue to record these fireside chats? What effect would they have had on the nation?

Transparency

The Persistence of Unemployment
Analyze fluctuations in unemployment during the period between 1929 and 1941.

1. Why would unemployment rates have been so low during 1929?
2. What are some possible causes of the surge in unemployment in 1938?

The Agricultural Adjustment Act (AAA) was another measure passed during the 100 Days. Among other steps to help the nation's farmers, the law sought to raise crop prices by reducing farm production. The Federal Emergency Relief Act gave money to state governments for programs to help the needy. The National Industrial Recovery Act protected workers and helped industry. It established the National Recovery Administration (NRA), to stimulate business, and the Public Works Administration (PWA), which put people to work building roads, bridges, schools, hospitals, and dams. Still, unemployment remained a serious problem.

By the summer of 1933, **more than three-fourths** of the banks closed in March had reopened. About 4,000 never did.

The Federal Deposit Insurance Corporation, created in 1933, provided **insurance for bank deposits** up to $2,500. The amount was raised to $5,000 in 1934.

An "Alphabet Soup"

Many of the government programs created during the New Deal were experiments. Roosevelt and his advisers were not certain how to bring the country out of the Depression. However, he was committed to trying new ideas. In the short term, that path focused on what he called relief, recovery, and reform. To relieve unemployment and put money in people's pockets, New Deal programs created jobs for the unemployed. That was expected to boost recovery, since people would have money to spend on goods that businesses and farms produced. The New Deal also promised to reform the existing financial system by setting up programs that would prevent similar depressions from happening again.

People referred to many of the New Deal programs by acronyms created from their three- or four-word names, for example, FHA for the Federal Housing Administration. The agencies were sometimes called Alphabet Soup Agencies. In a country where hungry people joked about eating "Hoover stew," a name given to the dish served to the poor in **soup kitchens**, people hoped Roosevelt's "alphabet soup" might provide the help they needed.

That aid included putting people back to work, which Roosevelt had said, in his **inaugural address**, was the government's "greatest primary task." The Civilian Conservation Corps (CCC) was established in 1933. By the time it ended in 1942, the CCC had provided jobs for 2.5 million men between the ages 18 and 25. They worked in parks and forests. Among their jobs was planting 3 billion trees on land at risk of drought

The Tennessee Valley Authority marked the first time the federal government was involved in energy production in the United States.

and dust storms, to prevent future Dust Bowl conditions. The men received shelter, clothing, three meals a day, and a salary of $30 per month, of which $25 was sent home to their families.

Another ambitious program established the TVA. This government agency hired jobless workers to build projects that transformed the lives of people living in the southeastern United States along the Tennessee River, one of the poorest parts of the nation. Dams and power stations built by the TVA improved flood control for area farmers and provided electricity for the first time to thousands of poor families, significantly improving their lives.

In addition to planting trees, the Civilian Conservation Corps dug canals, built wildlife shelters, and cleared campgrounds and beaches.

Roosevelt's Critics

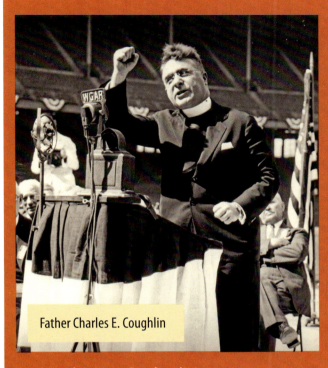

Father Charles E. Coughlin

Roosevelt's New Deal policies were attacked by critics on the political left and the right. On the left, some did not think government policies went far enough to help the poor. Huey Long, a Democratic senator from Louisiana, wanted a guaranteed minimum income for families and a major redistribution of wealth from the rich to the poor. Father Charles E. Coughlin, a Catholic priest from Detroit, Michigan, called for the **nationalization** of the banking system. His weekly radio show reached 30 million listeners.

The American Liberty League criticized Roosevelt from the right. The league denounced the New Deal as a **socialist** experiment and an attack on individual liberties. The group was led by wealthy business leaders. Some of them called Roosevelt, who was wealthy, a "traitor to his class."

TEACHER NOTES

📄 Document

Speech of Charles I. Dawson
Analyze a speech given by a member of the National Lawyers Committee of the American Liberty League on January 25, 1936.

1. What aspects of the New Deal does Dawson disagree with? Why would he take issue with these particular points?
2. What techniques does this speech use to sway a listener's viewpoint? How successful are these techniques?
3. What groups of people would have likely heard or read this speech? How might these different groups respond to its arguments?

🌐 Weblink

Three Essentials for Unemployment Relief
Examine President Roosevelt's 1933 statement to congress and the rationale that he used for the formation of the Civilian Conservation Corps.

1. What language does Roosevelt use to make the concept of the Civilian Conservation Corps more appealing to Congress? Why would this language have been effective?
2. What benefits does Roosevelt state that the creation of the corps would bring about? Why would he focus on these particular points?
3. How complete is Roosevelt's three-pronged plan? What else could the government do to assist the unemployed at this time?

Analyzing a Political Cartoon

Teacher Preplanning
Students will complete an analysis of a political comic or cartoon. An exemplary analysis will meet the following criteria.

- Identifies the cartoonist and source publication
- Describes the target audience of the cartoon
- Makes note of any titles or captions in the cartoon
- Outlines any individuals or institutions that appear in the cartoon
- Identifies symbols found in the cartoon and determines their meaning
- Notes the most important phrases or words used by the cartoonist
- Infers the emotions that the cartoonist is portraying or evoking
- Interprets and explains the message of the cartoon
- Records the different persuasive techniques used by the cartoonist
- Identifies how different groups would respond to the cartoon's message
- Presents information in a clear, concise manner
- Uses correct spelling, grammar, and punctuation

The Second New Deal and Social Security

Despite all efforts, the Depression continued during 1934. The unemployment rate was more than 21 percent, and many people who had jobs worked long hours for very low pay. Workers went on strike at companies throughout the country. The worst strike occurred in September, when hundreds of thousands of textile workers walked out at mills in the South and Northeast. In July 1935, Congress passed the National Labor Relations Act, also known as the Wagner Act, to help both employers and employees. It guaranteed workers the right to form unions.

In 1935, Roosevelt started work on what came to be called the Second New Deal,

with new measures to improve the economy. The Works Progress Administration (WPA), created in May, was one of the major new programs. It put millions to work building bridges, roads, and airports. Many WPA projects are still in use today, such as LaGuardia Airport in New York City, the Blue Ridge Parkway in North Carolina and Virginia, and the Griffith Observatory in Los Angeles. In addition, 5 percent of funding went to artists, writers, and theaters.

The Social Security Act, signed into law on August 14, 1935, is widely considered to be one of the most important pieces of legislation passed by the Roosevelt administration. By 1934, about 30 states

The National Guard was called to maintain order when textile workers went on strike in 1934. Violence broke out in some places, and a number of strikers were killed.

offered some form of **pension** to older people in need, but there was no such federal system. In addition, there was no **unemployment insurance** to help workers who had lost their jobs. Without retirement or unemployment benefits, people who could not find work or had retired from work had to rely on support from their family or community. Especially during the Depression, many families and local groups were unable to provide such aid.

Secretary of Labor Frances Perkins drafted, or wrote the first version of, the Social Security Act. The legislation set up a pension system, run by the federal government, for older people, and it provided benefits for the unemployed, the disabled, and orphans. Social Security remains an important source of benefits for Americans today.

Posters displayed during the 1930s gave Americans information about the new Social Security program.

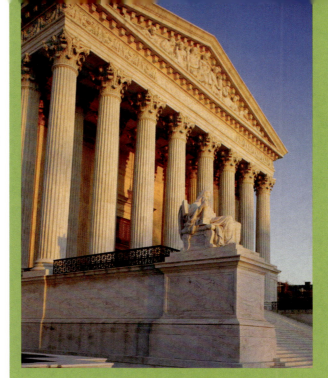

The Supreme Court and the New Deal

The Supreme Court did not always support Roosevelt and the New Deal. In 1935 and 1936, the Court ruled that the National Industrial Recovery Act and the Agricultural Adjustment Act were **unconstitutional**. Eventually, the Court found 11 New Deal laws to be unconstitutional.

Roosevelt feared that the Court would dismantle much of the New Deal. He developed a plan to change the membership of the Court by requiring judges who reached a certain age to retire and by increasing the number of judges. The president was harshly criticized for what was called his "court-packing" plan. Many people thought he should not interfere with another branch of government, and Congress did not pass the plan. It proved to be unnecessary because Court rulings in 1937 shifted in favor of the New Deal.

TEACHER NOTES

📄 Document

Supreme Court Political Cartoons
Examine the ways in which the news media responded to Roosevelt's issues with the Supreme Court.

1. What symbols and imagery are present in the cartoons? Why might these specific symbols have been chosen?
2. Do the cartoons take a pro-Roosevelt, pro-Supreme Court, or a neutral point of view? How do they illustrate this?
3. What aspects of Roosevelt's conflict do the cartoons focus on? Why would these aspects be highlighted?

👁 First Hand

An African American (Eugenia Martin) and the WPA
Explore excerpts from an African American woman's account of finding work with the WPA.

1. Why might people working WPA jobs have been stigmatized?
2. What kind of projects did the WPA enroll people in? Why might these particular jobs have been created?
3. What are some possible reasons for releasing people who had spent more than 18 months working WPA jobs?

Saving the Soil

Laws regulating banks and the stock market, as well as the establishment of Social Security, were meant to prevent problems that led to the Great Depression from occurring again. However, some of the New Deal's most important preventive actions affected agriculture. They had their greatest impact in the Great Plains states where much of the nation's food is grown.

Soon after drought conditions and Dust Bowl storms began, scientists realized that certain farming practices were partly responsible for turning valuable soil to dust across the region. Agricultural methods of the 1920s intended to grow as much food as possible had destroyed native grasses that held the soil in place in certain areas. Even land that could support crops only in times of above-average rainfall was cultivated in

The Soil Conservation Service set up a number of projects to study and develop practices to help save the soil, such as plowing in patterns.

the 1920s to boost food production. Besides planting trees, Civilian Conservation Corps workers reseeded native grasses on some former cropland.

The Soil Conservation Service (SCS) was established in 1935. Set up within the Department of Agriculture, the SCS used workers provided by the Civilian Conservation Corps, Civil Works Administration, and Works Progress Administration. These people worked with farmers to help them rebuild the soil and improve their farming practices. The SCS taught farmers how to plow their fields in patterns that could help hold moisture on the land, even in times of drought. Farmers also learned why it

is sometimes better to leave some land unplanted periodically, so that soil nutrients crops need could be rebuilt, instead of planting crops every year. The SCS operated research stations to investigate the extent and causes of soil erosion, as well as ways to prevent it.

The SCS was based on the idea that the federal government was ultimately responsible on a permanent basis for ensuring the health of one of the country's most valuable economic resources, its agricultural land. As Roosevelt wrote in a letter to state governors, "the nation that destroys its soil destroys itself." Three years after the SCS was established, soil erosion in the nation had decreased by 65 percent.

TEACHER NOTES

⬢ Transparency
A Long-Lasting Drought
Analyze climate information from time periods before and after the events of the Great Depression.

1. What other aspects of life in the United States would these droughts affect? How?
2. How would dry years before and after the Great Depression have impacted the nation? How does this compare to the dry years during the Depression? What would account for the differences between the dry years that occurred during the Great Depression and those that occurred outside of this time frame?

🌐 Weblink
Hugh Hammond Bennett "Father of Soil Conservation"
Review a biography of Hugh Hammond Bennett and learn about his role in the formation of the Soil Conservation Service.

1. How would Bennett's background have prepared him to become the chief of the SCS?
2. How did Bennett's methods change over time? What factors may have contributed to these changes?
3. What can you infer about Bennett's personality? What role would his personality have played in his attempts to bring attention to the need for soil conservation?

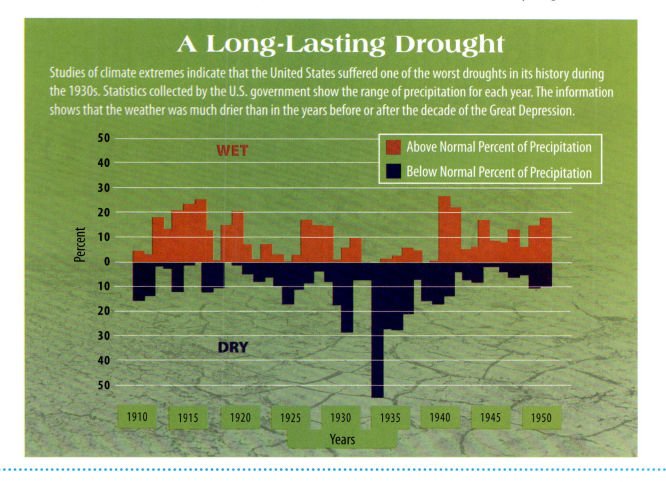

A Long-Lasting Drought

Studies of climate extremes indicate that the United States suffered one of the worst droughts in its history during the 1930s. Statistics collected by the U.S. government show the range of precipitation for each year. The information shows that the weather was much drier than in the years before or after the decade of the Great Depression.

WET

■ Above Normal Percent of Precipitation
■ Below Normal Percent of Precipitation

DRY

Percent

Years: 1910 1915 1920 1925 1930 1935 1940 1945 1950

Teacher Preplanning
Students will assess a letter and write an analysis. An exemplary analysis will meet the following criteria.

- Identifies the topic of the letter
- Determines the date on which the letter was written
- Identifies the main points and opinions expressed by the writer
- Determines any goals the writer is trying to accomplish with the letter
- Identifies the writer and recipient of the letter
- Presents background information about the writer and recipient
- Assesses the reliability of the letter's writer
- Analyzes any use of literary devices in the letter
- Differentiates between the facts and opinions stated by the writer of the letter
- Connects the letter to the societal and historical context in which it was written
- Infers additional information about the topic based on the content of the letter
- Uses a number of other resources to analyze the context in which the letter was written
- Uses correct spelling, grammar, and punctuation

Farm workers traveling from place to place looking for short-term jobs often had no choice but to live in tents. "Tent cities" became common in parts of the western United States.

At Home in Hooverville

Times were extremely difficult for many people during the Great Depression. People lost their businesses and jobs. Many lost their savings when banks failed. When people could not pay their rent, they lost their homes as well. Millions of homeless people settled in Hoovervilles, the name given to shantytowns where residents built shacks out of cardboard, wood, pieces of cloth, and tar paper. Inside the shacks, a small stove, some utensils, and something to sleep on could usually be found.

Hoovervilles were often situated near places where people could get free meals from charities. People stood in breadlines that were often blocks long. "Breadline" was the term used for a line of people waiting for any type of free food. As the Depression continued, governments as well as charities ran soup kitchens. If free meals were not available, men, women, and children searched through trash dumps and garbage cans looking for food.

Some Hoovervilles had families with children, while others were exclusively male. Some of the largest Hoovervilles, with thousands of residents, were located in or near large cities such as New York and Washington, D.C. The biggest Hooverville in New York was in Central Park in the borough of Manhattan, near a reservoir

The Hooverville at the reservoir in New York's Central Park was abandoned in 1933, when work on the reservoir was resumed.

 Document

May Gamble Young to City Council, April 24, 1937
Examine a request sent to the Seattle City Council requesting that the government remove the Hooverville that had been created in the city.

1. What arguments does the writer use to justify the need to remove the Hooverville? Why would she choose to focus on these points?
2. What tone does the letter take? What emotions can you conclude the writer is expressing in the document? Were her feelings toward the Hooverville justified? Why or why not?

 Video

Hooverville in Central Park
Examine an account of the formation of shantytowns in locations across the United States, such as Manhattan.

1. How did public perception of homeless individuals change over the course of the Great Depression? What factors may have influenced this?
2. Why were these villages named Hoovervilles? Was the name meant as a compliment? Why or why not?

on which work had been suspended. Stone blocks from the reservoir were used to build a structure that was 20 feet tall.

The state of Washington had dozens of Hoovervilles. One of the most notable was in Seattle. In existence from 1931 to 1941, it was started by a group of unemployed lumberjacks. The community, which set up its own form of local government, eventually held 1,500 men. Other Hoovervilles held only a few hundred people. A shantytown on the banks of the Mississippi River in St. Louis, Missouri, was home to about 500 people. It also had its own government and even set up its own churches.

Conditions in the settlements were grim. The unsanitary way of life posed health risks to residents and also those living nearby. Still, most people were sympathetic to those living in Hoovervilles.

Okies arriving in California often settled in Hoovervilles made up of tents. Some found work on corporate farms, where they dealt with fruit and vegetable crops instead of wheat. People who found work on these farms earned between $0.75 and $1.25 for each day of back-breaking labor picking crops. The workers were forced to pay $0.25 per day to live in a different type of Hooverville that was operated by companies that owned the farms. The structures were often shacks made of tar paper and had no plumbing, electricity, or floors. Some people were also forced to buy food for their families from a company-owned store.

Shortcomings of the New Deal

New Deal programs were costly for the federal government, which had a budget deficit each year. This means the amount of money the government spent was greater than the amount it collected in taxes. By 1937, the economy seemed to be improving, and as a result, the federal government sharply reduced spending to lower the deficit. However, the spending cuts had a negative effect on the economy, and many of the gains that had been made were lost. Conditions became worse. Industrial production and stock prices dropped, and unemployment rose. The downturn lasted through much of 1938.

By the next year, though, achievements could be seen. The New Deal had reformed the nation's banking system, put millions of unemployed Americans to work, and created Social Security to provide people in need with financial support, or what became known as a "safety net." The Fair Labor Standards Act, passed in 1938, established, for certain industries, a minimum wage of $0.25 per hour and a maximum work week of 44 hours. **Economic indicators** showed signs of recovery. Between 1933 and 1939, **gross domestic product** increased by about $35 billion. Purchases of consumer goods increased as more people had more money to spend, and private investment in industry rose.

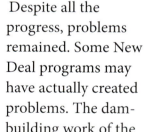

Women employees at a popular variety store went on strike for better working conditions in 1937. It was the first successful all-female sit-down strike in the United States.

Despite all the progress, problems remained. Some New Deal programs may have actually created problems. The dam-building work of the TVA sometimes flooded land that farmers had used to grow crops. The TVA paid the landowners for such land, but tenant farmers, who rented the land they worked, lost their livelihoods. Sharecroppers, who paid their rent by giving part of their crops to the landowner, were also affected.

The Agricultural Adjustment Act came under criticism because of some of its

The NRA established 557 basic codes, plus 227 supplementary codes, that affected millions of U.S. workers.

👁 **First Hand**

LeRoy Hankel – Participating in the AAA
Review a LeRoy Hankel's account of the AAA and the effect that it had on farmers.

1. What reason does Hankel give for some people staying out of the program? Why would this be a deciding factor? What advantages were there to not participating in the program? What were the disadvantages?
2. What conclusions can you draw about the priorities set by the AAA based on this interview?

🌐 **Weblink**

Fair Labor Standards Act of 1938: Maximum Struggle for a Minimum Wage
Examine the struggles faced by Roosevelt in his attempt to pass the controversial Fair Labor Standards Act.

1. Why would this act have been considered controversial? Who would most strongly object to it? Why?
2. How did the act change as it passed through Congress? Ultimately, can it be considered a success? Why or why not?

policies. To help increase the prices farmers received for their crops, the AAA paid farmers to grow less food, at a time when many Americans were hungry. Farmers were sometimes paid to plow under millions of acres of wheat, dump many gallons of milk, or destroy livestock.

The National Recovery Administration was supposed to establish codes of fair business practices within different industries. The codes were drawn up by representatives from business, labor, and government. The NRA successfully raised wages and outlawed child labor, but businesses dominated the industry groups, and the codes often favored them. On the other hand, some companies charged that rules passed about wages, working hours, and workplace safety restricted their ability to operate efficiently and interfered with economic recovery.

In the end, critics of New Deal programs said Roosevelt's approach to solving problems doubled the nation's debt without narrowing the gap between rich and poor. In addition, although New Deal public works programs provided jobs for millions of people, unemployment remained high. It still stood at 17 percent in 1939.

The Fair Labor Standards Act set the **minimum working age** at 14 for after-school hours and 16 for during-school hours.

In 1933, the AAA paid farmers to destroy **6 million pigs**.

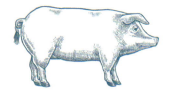

Analyzing a Magazine Article

Discriminatory Practices

African Americans may have suffered more than any other group during the Great Depression. Throughout the United States at the time, and especially in the South, African Americans faced many types of discrimination. Often, they could not live in certain areas, attend the best schools, or be employed in higher-paying occupations. Poorly educated and working in low-paying jobs before the Depression began, large numbers of African Americans found life extremely difficult in the 1930s.

Prior to Franklin Roosevelt's presidency, many African Americans had voted for Republican candidates. This was partly out of respect for Abraham Lincoln, the Republican president who ended slavery in the Civil War, and partly because the leading politicians in the South were Democrats. That voting pattern changed in the 1930s, even though some of Roosevelt's actions did little to help African Americans. In 1935, for example, Roosevelt failed to support a federal law against **lynching**. The president said he could not support the bill because Southern voters were against it and some Southern members of Congress would have retaliated by voting against his New Deal policies.

In addition, some New Deal programs had discriminatory practices. The Civilian Conservation Corps and Tennessee

The Farm Security Administration was a New Deal agency set up to help poor rural citizens, including African Americans. One FSA program helped farmers obtain loans to buy land, livestock, or equipment.

Valley Authority both had segregated work camps, or separate camps for white and black workers. The policy of the Agricultural Adjustment Administration to pay landowners not to plant crops also hurt African Americans, since many were **migrant workers**, tenant farmers, or sharecroppers. Thousands of African Americans were forced to leave the land. Many of them moved to Northern cities, where unemployment among African Americans was more than 50 percent.

Discrimination against African Americans was widespread in the National Recovery Administration. In some states, the NRA allowed companies to offer white people the first chance at jobs and to pay African Americans lower wages. In some places, the NRA did not stop companies from firing African-American employees to give their jobs to white people.

In the 1930s, the Social Security program did not include some types of jobs in agriculture and domestic work that were largely filled by African Americans. As a result, many African Americans could not receive benefits. Agencies such as the Federal Housing Administration had different rules for African Americans. The FHA was set up to help Americans obtain **mortgages** to buy homes. In general, the agency gave banks guarantees that the government would pay mortgage loans if the homeowners could not afford to continue making payments. However, the FHA did not guarantee mortgages for African Americans who tried to buy homes in white neighborhoods.

Mexican Americans during the Depression

The Great Depression was also a hard time for Mexican Americans. Farm owners and business managers tended to favor hiring non-Hispanic workers, whom they considered "more American." Many Mexican Americans found it difficult to obtain employment.

Some local governments, as well as the federal government, adopted what were known as repatriation policies, sending people to Mexico rather than providing them assistance under government programs. People were offered free train rides to Mexico if they chose to go. The Federal Bureau of Immigration and local officials also rounded up more than 400,000 people and sent them to Mexico. These people included immigrants from Mexico who had become American citizens and U.S. citizens of Mexican descent who had been born in the United States.

TEACHER NOTES

📖 Document

Mexican American Documents
Examine accounts of the challenges facing Mexican Americans during the Great Depression.

1. How does Carey McWilliams show the issues facing Mexicans and Mexican Americans? What methods does he use to illustrate these issues?
2. What tone is used in the Mexican Consulate's letter? Why might the Mexican government want to encourage people repatriation?
3. What factors might have caused or contributed to the changing views on Mexicans and Mexican Americans in the southwestern states? Why would the government see repatriation as the best option?

👁 First Hand

A Letter From Eleanor Roosevelt
Assess a response from the First Lady to the NAACP about the difficulties of enacting an anti-lynching law.

1. What reasons does Eleanor Roosevelt give for the impossibility of enacting such a law? Why would these reasons prevent it?
2. How might her intended audience view this letter? How might other political groups interpret her response?

Analyzing a Historical Video

Teacher Preplanning

Students will watch and assess a video related to a historical event, and write an analysis of the video. An exemplary video analysis will meet the following criteria.

- Identifies the purpose of the video
- Identifies the intended audience of the video
- Describes how the content of the video is presented
- Summarizes the information and opinions presented in the video
- Analyzes the quality of the content presented in the video
- Assesses the effectiveness of the video
- Determines whether the images and graphics used in the video relate to the content
- Determines whether the video is easy to follow and understand
- Gives the analysis a clear and consistent purpose
- Organizes the analysis in a logical, effective manner
- Presents a strong, clear argument about the video
- Provides strong and accurate details to support the argument about the video
- Considers other perspectives on the purpose and effectiveness of the video
- Makes connections between the video and the novel
- Properly integrates quotations from the video
- Cites all sources used in the analysis

When World War II began, many Americans found work in factories, where they produced guns, ammunition, tanks, planes, and ships.

The Depression Ends

The Great Depression finally ended in 1939 because of a number of reasons. New Deal policies and agencies had injected large amounts of government money into the economy, put millions of people back to work, and changed the regulation of banks and other businesses to reduce risky practices. The drought that had plagued much of the country ended, making conditions better for farmers.

Nevertheless, the primary reason for the end of the Depression may have been events overseas. Beginning in the mid-1930s, German leader Adolf Hitler had been building up his country's armed forces and seizing territory from nearby countries, as had Italy and Japan. These developments raised the possibility of war. The United States responded with an official policy of **neutrality**. However, at the same time, the U.S. government began to increase military spending to strengthen national defense in case a war occurred.

In September 1939, World War II began in Europe when Germany invaded Poland, and France and Great Britain responded by declaring war on Germany. The United States, although still officially neutral, sold many types of goods to Great Britain. In 1940, Roosevelt was elected president for a third time, something no president had ever done before. Then, as Germany defeated France and seemed to be preparing to invade Great Britain, the president convinced Congress to fund further strengthening of the U.S. military. The United States also instituted a **draft**, which reduced the number of young men seeking employment. The next year, Congress passed the Lend-Lease Act. Under this legislation, the United States provided ships, weapons, and other military supplies to Great Britain. This all served to put a growing number of Americans to work in war-related industries. Between 1939 and 1940, unemployment dropped from about 17 to 14 percent. Approximately 8 million people were still unemployed, but more and more were finding work. Other economic indicators, such as increases in the gross domestic product and private investment, also showed that recovery was under way.

Japan attacked the U.S. naval base at Pearl Harbor, Hawai'i, on December 7, 1941. Roosevelt called it "a date which will live in infamy" in a speech the next day asking Congress to declare war on Japan. The president's address to Congress was broadcast on radio nationwide. Three days later, Germany and Italy declared war on the United States.

The Japanese attack on Pearl Harbor killed 2,388 Americans and wounded 1,178, in addition to destroying or damaging hundreds of U.S. planes and dozens of ships.

World War II effectively ended the Depression. Factories went back to full production, turning out supplies for the war effort such as planes, tanks, and weapons. Farms were called upon to grow food for those overseas. Men enlisted in the armed forces, and women took jobs that would otherwise have gone to men, further reducing unemployment. By 1941, the unemployment rate had fallen to under 10 percent.

More than **62 million people** heard Roosevelt's fireside chat on December 9, 1941, in which he prepared the nation for going to war.

In 1941, the U.S. unemployment rate was 9.7 percent. By 1942, it had dropped to **4.7 percent**.

TEACHER NOTES

 Document

The Neutrality Act of 1935
Review the 1935 acts intended to prevent the United States from becoming involved in another World War.

1. What areas of commerce does the act focus on? Why might this be the case?
2. Why would the U.S. government wish to ensure neutrality? What factors would have contributed to this mindset?

 Video

Lend-Lease
Examine the events that led to the creation of the Lend-Lease Act.

1. Why would Congress have opposed the donation of military equipment to Great Britain? Why would President Roosevelt have been in favor of it? What factors may have caused this difference of opinion?
2. How did President Roosevelt sell this notion? Why would this "nonsense" have been successful?

Analyzing an Interview

Teacher Preplanning
Students will listen to and assess an interview related to a historical or cultural event, and write an analysis of what they have learned. An exemplary interview analysis will meet the following criteria.

- Identifies where and when the interview took place
- Identifies the subject of the interview
- Describes how the interview is presented
- Gives examples of the information provided by the interview
- Summarizes the information and opinions presented by the subject of the interview
- States whether the information is a firsthand or secondhand account
- Points out how easy or difficult to understand the subject of the interview is
- Organizes the analysis in a logical, effective manner
- Makes inferences about the experiences of the interview subject
- Compares the interview to other sources about the same event
- Cites all sources used in the analysis
- Uses correct spelling, grammar, and punctuation

The Aftermath of the Great Depression

The United States went from the Great Depression immediately into World War II. Americans had united in the 1930s to deal with economic hardship. They came together in the 1940s in the effort to win the war. Already familiar with the concept of "making do," people were willing to make sacrifices for the war effort, such as limits on the amount of food and gasoline they could buy. Americans collected scrap metal and rubber, to be recycled and used to produce arms, and they bought war bonds from the government to help pay for the high cost of war. People planted "victory gardens" to grow fruits and vegetables for their own use.

A large network of government agencies was needed to coordinate wartime actions. As a result of the New Deal, the country was already familiar with the notion of economic planning and cooperation. Instead of New Deal agencies, the country now had such organizations as the Office of War Mobilization and National War Labor Board.

The number of women in the U.S. work force increased from 5.1 million in 1939 to more than 7.25 million in 1943.

The war caused significant changes in the lives of women, African Americans, and unionized workers. Women were now working in large numbers and taking responsibility for the income of their families. In many ways, this laid the basis for the women's rights movement that began in the 1960s. African Americans also saw advances, with opportunities to serve in the military or gain better employment. The power of unions also increased, as the output of factory workers gained in importance during the war.

The United States in the early 1940s was fundamentally different in many ways from the nation at the beginning of the Depression. The **infrastructure** of the nation had been transformed. Perhaps even more significantly, the federal government's relationship to the people had changed. Previously, Americans had not expected the federal government to provide for them. Now, though, expectations had changed, and the government from this point on would play a major role in people's lives. The role of the president, the size of government, and its level of engagement with the people all grew as a result of the Great Depression.

Through programs such as Social Security, the federal government would now provide a safety net for its citizens. The government would insure people's bank deposits, regulate the stock market, and oversee the prices paid to farmers. Americans had been through a time of great hardship. Many people emerged from the Depression trusting that the government would take care of them if another catastrophe occurred.

Making the Best of Hard Times

Most people in the United States managed to get through the hard times of the Great Depression. Families grew closer and spent more time together. In addition, people found inexpensive ways to entertain themselves and temporarily escape from the difficulties they faced. Some of those ways are still popular.

By the time the Depression ended, more than 28 million American households owned a radio, and listening to music, sports, news, and Roosevelt's fireside chats was a shared experience. Radio soap operas attracted regular listeners, as did shows featuring heroes such as the Lone Ranger and The Shadow. The importance of radio for news and entertainment was in many ways similar to the role of television or the internet today.

Millions of people went to the movies each week. Some of the films of the 1930s are still popular today, such as *Gone with the Wind* and *The Wizard of Oz*, both released in 1939. Two years before that, Walt Disney released its first full-length animated feature film, *Snow White and the Seven Dwarfs*. The film was a success, and since then, Disney has made numerous full-length animated movies.

In the 1930s, an unemployed engineer created the board game Monopoly. The goal of the game was to buy property, put up buildings, and get rich. By 1935, by which time Parker Brothers had acquired the game, Monopoly was the most popular game in the country. It has remained popular ever since.

TEACHER NOTES

First Hand
Interviews With Moviegoers
Observe firsthand accounts of the film industry's influence and popularity during the 1930s.

1. Based on the interviews, why was the film industry so popular during this time? What evidence supports this?
2. What was an audience looking to get out of the movies? How would this compare to other forms of entertainment at the time?
3. How does the moviegoing experience today differ from that of someone in the 1930s? Are there any similarities?

Weblink
War Production
Analyze the effects that the Second World War had on the economy of the United States.

1. What mindset fueled the American system of production during World War II? How would this have affected the economy?
2. How would the economy of the United States during World War II compare to the economy during the Roaring Twenties and the Great Depression? How would they be they similar? What differences would exist? Why?

Researching for a Writing Assignment

Teacher Preplanning

Students will complete a thorough research process to prepare for a writing assignment, and organize their research in a logical manner that supports their writing. An exemplary research process will meet the following criteria.

- Creates a goal for the research, based on the topic and thesis
- Creates specific, thoughtful, and inventive research questions that are relevant to the topic
- Uses high-quality sources that pertain to the topic and come in a variety of formats, such as books, primary sources, websites, and databases
- Determines the accuracy of all sources used
- Uses sources that provide balanced research and various perspectives of the topic in question
- Takes notes to highlight the key facts and ideas in order to answer all research questions
- Extracts relevant, detailed information from the sources during the note-taking process
- Writes notes in the student's own words
- Organizes the research notes logically and in a way that sets up the information and ideas for analysis and the writing process
- Analyzes the information and produces ideas and points to support the working thesis
- Uses an effective and suitable format to present all research
- Properly cites all sources used
- Uses quotations properly and ethically

Before and After

During the Great Depression, many people endured significant hardship. Laws that were passed and policies that were adopted during the period did much to promote economic recovery. Many laws and policies were directed at financial and social reform.

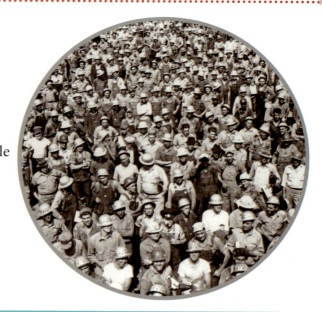

Social Security

Before	After

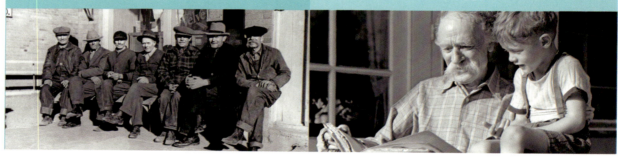

The Stock Market

Before	After

Home Ownership

Before	After

Insurance of Bank Deposits

Before	After

Farm Loans

Before	After

Conducting an Interview

Teacher Preplanning

Students will prepare for and conduct an interview with a person who has experienced a notable event. An exemplary interview will meet the following criteria.

- Demonstrates background knowledge of the subject
- Prepares a comprehensive list of questions before conducting the interview
- Successfully develops a rapport with the subject
- Makes eye contact with and speaks clearly to the subject
- Uses an appropriate, polite manner when conducting the interview
- Asks and clarifies appropriate questions
- Encourages the subject to expand upon topics in greater detail
- Asks relevant follow-up questions
- Records statements made by the subject clearly and accurately
- Explains the subject's views in detail
- Relates the topics addressed in the interview to the chosen event
- Presents the interview in a clear, concise manner

Quiz

1 Who were the three Republican presidents elected in the 1920s?

2 What was the name given to October 29, 1929?

3 What did people call the shantytowns where poor people settled during the Depression?

4 What government agency was created to build dams and power stations, improve flood control, and provide electrical power for people living near the Tennessee River?

5 When was the Social Security Act signed into law?

6 Who was the secretary of labor during the time Franklin Roosevelt was president?

7 What was the minimum wage set by the Fair Labor Standards Act?

8 What was the term used for people who traveled to California to escape the Dust Bowl?

9 When did the drought that led to the Dust Bowl begin in the central United States?

10 What did Roosevelt call December 7, 1941?

1. Warren G. Harding, Calvin Coolidge, and Herbert Hoover 2. Black Tuesday 3. Hoovervilles 4. The Tennessee Valley Authority 5. August 14, 1935 6. Frances Perkins 7. $0.25 per hour 8. Okies 9. Summer 1930 10. A date which will live in infamy

Be a Historian

History is the written record of the lives of people who have lived in the past. Historians research these records and share their findings with others so everyone is enriched by the experiences of people and events that have shaped the world.

Think about an event in the past 25 years that you would like to know more about. This can be a major event in the world, or it may be something that happened in the place where you live. Write down six questions about this time. You may want to know what it was like to live at this time or how the event changed the way people lived.

Find a person who lived during this time that you can interview about the event. Begin by recording your name, the date of the interview, the name and birth date of the person you are interviewing, as well as any other important information, such as the names of his or her spouse and children. Then, ask the six questions you wrote down earlier. Record the responses. Be sure to accurately quote every word.

You have created a historic record. Consider the answers you received to your questions. Does the information you gathered cause you to view this event differently? What new things did you learn?

Key Words

administration: the activities of running the federal government associated with the president

cabinet: a group of advisers to the president that includes the heads of federal departments

consumer goods: products that are purchased by people for their personal use

defaulted: failed to fulfill an obligation, such as repaying a loan

deposited: put money into a bank account

draft: mandatory enlistment in the armed services

drought: a long period of lower than average rainfall

dust storm: a thick cloud of dust carried over a large area by high winds

economic indicators: statistics that indicate how well a country's or area's economy is performing

economy: the wealth and resources of a country or area

executive orders: orders from the president to government agencies that the president has the authority to issue under powers granted to him or her by the U.S. Constitution

foreclosed: took property because an individual could not make loan payments

gross domestic product: the total value of the goods and services a country produces

inaugural address: the speech given by a president when he or she is inaugurated, or sworn into office

infrastructure: the facilities and structures needed for the operation of a society, such as buildings, roads, and bridges

lynching: killing someone, especially by a mob, for something allegedly done but without a legal trial

migrant workers: people who move from place to place to do seasonal work

minimum wage: the lowest wage permitted by law

mortgages: loans from banks to buy a house

nationalization: action by a government to take control of an industry away from private companies

neutrality: a position of not taking sides in a conflict

pension: money paid on a regular basis to someone who is no longer working

prosperity: a time of success

public works programs: government projects that employ workers to build structures for the public good

recession: a time of decline in economic activity

socialist: someone who believes in socialism, a system in which the government controls production of goods

soup kitchens: places where poor people could obtain free food

stock market: a system for buying and selling stocks, or shares of the ownership of a company

surplus: an amount greater than what is needed

tariff: a tax on goods coming into a country

unconstitutional: government actions not permitted under the U.S. Constitution

unemployment insurance: payments to unemployed workers for a period of time to help them pay their bills while they seek new jobs

unemployment rate: the percentage of workers who want but cannot find jobs and are out of work

Index

LIGHTB▲X

✚ SUPPLEMENTARY RESOURCES

Click on the plus icon ✚ found in the bottom left corner of each spread to open additional teacher resources.

- Download and print the book's quizzes and activities
- Access curriculum correlations
- Explore additional web applications that enhance the Lightbox experience

LIGHTBOX DIGITAL TITLES
Packed full of integrated media

VIDEOS

INTERACTIVE MAPS

WEBLINKS

SLIDESHOWS
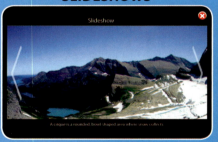

QUIZZES

OPTIMIZED FOR

✓ **TABLETS**

✓ **WHITEBOARDS**

✓ **COMPUTERS**

✓ **AND MUCH MORE!**

Published by Smartbook Media Inc.
350 5th Avenue, 59th Floor New York, NY 10118
Website: www.openlightbox.com

Project Coordinator: Heather Kissock
Designer: Mandy Christiansen

Library of Congress Cataloging-in-Publication Data
Names: Gregory, Joy. | Willis, John, 1989 -author
Title: The Great Depression / Joy Gregory and John Willis.
Description: New York, NY : Smartbook Media Inc., 2017. | Series: U.S. history | Includes bibliographical references and index.
Identifiers: LCCN 2016013730 (print) | LCCN 2016014141 (ebook) | ISBN 9781510512863 (hard cover : alkaline paper) | ISBN 9781510512870 (Multi-user ebook)
Subjects: LCSH: United States--History--1933-1945--Juvenile literature. | United States--History--1919-1933--Juvenile literature. | Depressions, 1929--United States--Juvenile literature. | New Deal, 1933-1939--Juvenile literature. | United States--Economic conditions--1918-1945--Juvenile literature.
Classification: LCC E806 .G835 2017 (print) | LCC E806 (ebook) | DDC 973.91--dc23

LC record available at http://lccn.loc.gov/2016013730

Printed in Brainerd, Minnesota, United States
1 2 3 4 5 6 7 8 9 0 20 19 18 17 16

072016
150716

Every reasonable effort has been made to trace ownership and to obtain permission to reprint copyright material. The publisher would be pleased to have any errors or omissions brought to its attention so that they may be corrected in subsequent printings. The publisher acknowledges Getty Images, iStock, Corbis, and Alamy as its primary image suppliers for this title.